Mozart: 59 Fascinating Facts For Kids

Andrew Gibbs

This book is just one of a series of "Fascinating Facts For Kids" books. For more fascinating facts about people, history, animals, and much more please visit:

www.fascinatingfactsforkids.com

Contents

Introduction

Wolfgang Amadeus Mozart was probably the most gifted musician who has ever lived, having a musical talent that can only be dreamed of.

He was not only a great composer, but also a great pianist and he astonished the audiences of his time with his skills.

Unlike some composers, Mozart had no interest in developing new types of music, but just wanted to write as close to perfection as possible. Many people would argue that he achieved perfection.

But in spite of his astonishing gifts, Mozart was just a human being like the rest of us. He could be arrogant and rude, and was not a particularly attractive man.

But he wrote music unlike anything that had been heard before and it is still admired today, over 200 years since he died.

I hope the following facts will fascinate you and encourage you to find out even more about Mozart and his wonderful music.

Andrew Gibbs
October 2014

Early Life

1. Wolfgang Amadeus Mozart was born on January 27, 1756, in the Austrian town of Salzburg.

2. Wolfgang and his elder sister, Maria Anna, were the only surviving children of Leopold and Anna Maria Mozart.

3. Leopold Mozart was a fine musician, being an excellent violinist, teacher, and composer, who played in the orchestra of the Archbishop of Salzburg.

Leopold Mozart

4.   Both Wolfgang and his sister showed a talent for music, but Leopold soon realized that his son's musical abilities were exceptional.

5.   Leopold taught music to both his children. Wolfgang learned keyboard and violin, and by the age of just five he was performing in public and had written his first composition.

Leopold and his children

A Tour of Europe

6. Leopold realized that money could be made from his remarkable children and in 1762, when Wolfgang was just six years old, they set off on a tour of Europe.

Six-year-old Mozart

7. Wolfgang and his sister spent the next eleven years visiting the great cities of Europe, showing off their musical talents to the royalty and nobility of many different countries.

8. Wolfgang was a charming child and enchanted everyone who met him, including the Emperor and Empress of Austria. The Emperor was so impressed with Wolfgang that he called him his "little magician."

9. While traveling through Europe, Wolfgang was able to hear every kind of music from composers of many different countries, which gave him ideas to use in his own music.

10. As well as performing, Wolfgang was also writing music while traveling, and by the age of fourteen he had written over 100 compositions, including symphonies, concertos, and operas. Even at such a young age he was establishing his reputation as a composer, and becoming famous throughout Europe.

11. A symphony is a piece of music written for orchestra, usually in four separate sections, or "movements," and Mozart was to become one of the most important composers of this type of music.

12. Mozart wrote 41 symphonies during his lifetime, but it was between the ages of fourteen and eighteen that he wrote most of them. In this four year period he wrote an astonishing 27 symphonies.

13. Although Wolfgang had already written two operas which had been performed in Austria, Leopold knew that to be really judged a success he must write an opera for Italy.

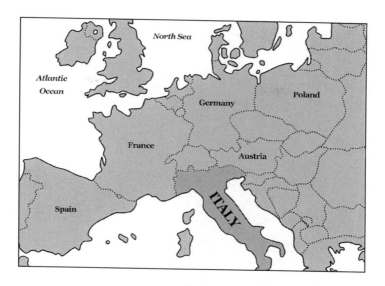

14. At the time, Italy was the home of opera, and in 1770 the Mozarts visited the country and put on Wolfgang's new opera, called "Mitridate." The Italians didn't believe a fourteen-year-old Austrian boy could write an Italian opera, but at the first rehearsal there was a storm of applause. "Mitridate" went on to be performed twenty-one times and, to Leopold's delight, it made a great deal of money.

15. Although the European tour was a great success, making Wolfgang's name widely known as a musician and composer of extraordinary ability, the constant traveling had an effect on the health of the boy. He was often ill and on one occasion came close to death.

Paris

16. By 1773, Mozart began to travel less and spend more time at home in Salzburg. But it was difficult to find well-paid work as a musician and so, in 1778, Mozart and his mother left for Paris.

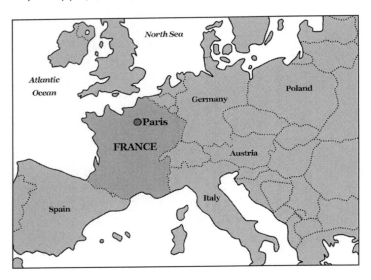

17. Paris, the capital of France, was one the great musical cities of Europe. The idea was to find a job there, after which the rest of the family would join Wolfgang and his mother.

18. Mozart knew that to be successful in France he had to write popular music that the people of Paris would love. He did just that with his 31st symphony, called the "Paris Symphony."

19. The night before the first performance, though, Mozart heard the musicians rehearsing his new work and thought they sounded awful. He decided not to go to the next day's concert.

20. But the following day he changed his mind and was delighted when the symphony was cheered by the audience. The "Paris Symphony" became so popular that it was to receive many performances over the following years.

21. But despite this success, the trip to Paris turned out to be a disaster. Twenty-two-year-old Wolfgang didn't like the city, and spent much more money than he received. He also suffered a personal tragedy when his mother was taken ill. She was not to recover, and in July 1778, Anna Maria Mozart died at the age of just fifty-seven.

Anna Maria Mozart, Wolfgang's mother

Back to Salzburg

22.   Mozart was heart-broken by his mother's death and he dealt with his grief by writing music. He stayed in Paris until the following year when, after being unable to find a job in the French capital, he returned to Salzburg to play the violin in the court orchestra.

23.   But Mozart was not happy in Salzburg, as he knew he should be doing something better than playing in an orchestra. But his growing reputation as a composer led to him being asked to write a new opera for the German city of Munich.

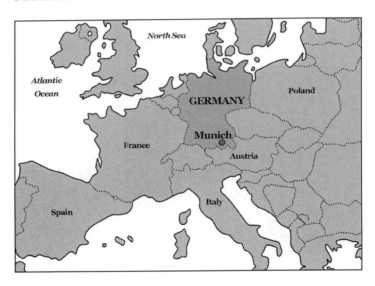

24.   The opera was to be called "Idomeneo" and was based on an old legend about an ancient

Greek king. If it was a success Mozart hoped to be offered a job in Munich.

25. "Idomeneo" was not only the finest work that Mozart had written so far, but it was also the finest opera that had ever been written.

26. Unfortunately, no offer of a job came from the success of "Idomeneo," but Mozart was determined to leave Salzburg.

27. Mozart was convinced that Vienna, the capital city of Austria, would give him more opportunities to earn a living as a musician than Salzburg. As well as composing, he could teach and play in concerts.

Vienna

28. At the time, Vienna was transforming itself into a major artistic and musical center of Europe, and in 1781, Mozart left his job in Salzburg and set off for the Austrian capital.

29. Mozart loved Vienna and began to organise concerts at which he played his own compositions. He became very successful at this, and put on over seventy concerts in five years, often playing as the soloist in his own piano concertos.

30. A piano concerto is a composition featuring a solo piano accompanied by an orchestra. Mozart wrote these concertos in a new and exciting way and he dazzled the audiences with his playing.

31. Mozart wrote 27 piano concertos in all, and

to this day they are considered some of the finest music ever written.

32.   Mozart knew that to become really successful in Vienna he had to write an opera and it had to be written in German, the language of Austria. Most operas up until then had been written in the Italian language.

33.   The Emperor of Austria, who was a great supporter of the arts and music, asked Mozart to write a German opera, which was to be called "Die Entführung aus dem Serail."

34.   This new opera had its first performance in July 1782, and it was a great success, earning Mozart money and making his name well-known in Vienna.

35.   There was some slight criticism from the Emperor though, who complained to Mozart that his new opera had too many notes, to which Mozart replied, "There are just as many notes as there should be!"

Marriage

36. In 1782, Wolfgang married a young singer called Constanza Weber, much to the disappointment of his father, who thought his son could have found someone better to marry than a common singer!

Constanza Weber

37. Wolfgang and Constanza were to have six children during their marriage, although as was common in those days, not all of them survived through childhood. The only two that lived for more than a year were Karl and Franz.

Karl and Franz Mozart

Meeting Haydn

38.   The greatest composer of the time was
Joseph Haydn, and when he visited Vienna in
1785, Mozart invited him to his home where
Haydn was played three string quartets that
Wolfgang had recently written.

Joseph Haydn

39.   A string quartet is a piece of music, usually
in four separate movements, written for two
violins, a viola, and a cello. Haydn was one of the
first composers to write for the string quartet
and was a master at using this combination of
instruments.

Haydn playing in a string quartet

40.   On hearing Mozart's new string quartets, Haydn was so impressed that he said to Leopold Mozart, who was visiting his son, "I swear to you before God and as an honest man, that your son is the greatest composer I know either personally or by reputation."

Fame & Money

41. By the 1780s, Mozart had achieved wealth and fame, and he and Constanza were able to move into a big, new apartment in the center of Vienna.

42. Mozart was now earning good money but neither he nor Constanza were very good at keeping it. The rent on their apartment was expensive, they employed servants, and Wolfgang spent a lot of money on a billiard table! This was the start of the money problems that Constanza and Wolfgang would have in later years.

43. It was in their new apartment that Mozart wrote some of his greatest masterpieces, including piano concertos, string quartets, and perhaps his most popular opera, "The Marriage of Figaro."

44. "The Marriage of Figaro" is a comedy and had a certain amount of success in Vienna, but when it was performed in the city of Prague, it was a tremendous success. Mozart was now the most popular composer in Europe.

45. The people of Prague loved Mozart's music, and he wrote a symphony and another opera for the city. The opera, "Don Giovanni," was the complete opposite to "The Marriage of Figaro," being a serious and dramatic work, and unlike any opera that had been heard before.

Money Problems

46.   When Mozart returned to Vienna in 1787, the city was not as wealthy as it had been, which meant that Mozart struggled to find paid work as a composer. Mozart soon found himself without any money, in debt, and in a serious financial situation.

47.   Despite the changes to his life, he still managed to compose some of the greatest music ever written during these desperate times.

48.   By 1791, Mozart's fortunes had begun to pick up a little and his career as a composer began to improve.

49.   In September 1791, Mozart's new opera, "The Magic Flute" opened. This too was a great success, being seen by massive audiences and being performed hundreds of times.

50.   Mozart was now at the height of his powers, and wealthy people were again paying him to write music for them. He and Constanza were always short of money, though, having no idea about organizing their finances.

The Last Year

51.   1791 was to be the last year of Mozart's life, and he was to write some of his finest music. As well as "The Magic Flute," he also composed his last piano concerto and a clarinet concerto.

52.   At the time, the clarinet was a fairly new instrument, and Mozart wrote his concerto for a clarinet virtuoso called Anton Stadler. The instrument has a warm, rich sound which Mozart used to great effect in one of his most beautiful compositions.

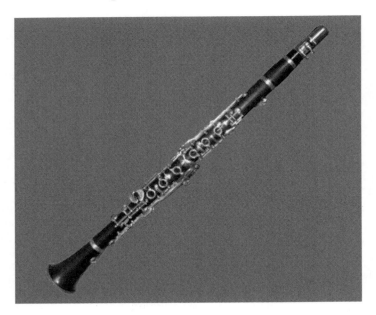

The clarinet

53.   One piece of music he was asked to write was quite unusual. A mysterious stranger called on Mozart and asked him to write a Requiem Mass, which is a piece of music that honors the dead. The stranger brought a letter with him which promised Mozart a lot of money if he would accept the job.

54.   Mozart thought that this stranger had come from another world, and that the Requiem he would write would be honoring his own death.

55.   Mozart began work on his Requiem but was not to finish it. He was not in the best of health at this time, and by November he had become seriously ill and close to death.

Mozart's Death

56. Mozart died on December 5, 1791, at the age of just thirty-five and on hearing of his death, Joseph Haydn declared, "The world will not see such a talent again for a hundred years."

"Mozart's Last Days" - a painting by Hermann von Kaulbach

57. Mozart had very little money when he died and could only be given the cheapest possible funeral.

58. The site of Mozart's grave is not known, but fifty years after he died, a statue of the great composer was put up in the Salzburg, the city of his birth.

Salzburg's statue of Mozart

59. The Requiem was completed not long after Mozart's death by Franz Süssmayr, a friend of Mozart and a fellow composer, and it is still performed to this day.

Conclusion

Mozart's short life was often one of illness and lack of money, but in spite of these problems he wrote some of the greatest music the world has known.

In his thirty-five years on Earth he wrote over 600 compositions, including 41 symphonies, 22 operas, and 27 piano concertos. These numbers would have been even greater had he not died at such a young age.

He was a supremely gifted musician and his wonderful music, which seemed to flow easily from him, is still enjoyed and marveled at by people from all over the world to this day.

Illustration Attributions

Title page
Barbara Krafft [Public domain]
{{PD-1923}}

Leopold Mozart
Pietro Antonio Lorenzoni (*1721, †1782) [Public domain]
{{PD-1923}}

Leopold and his children
Jean-Baptiste Delafosse [Public domain]
{{PD-1923}}

Six-year-old Mozart
AnonymousUnknown author, possibly by Pietro Antonio Lorenzoni (1721-1782) [Public domain]
{{PD-1923}}

Anna Maria Mozart, Wolfgang's mother
Rosa Hagenauer-Barducci (1744-1809) [Public domain]
{{PD-1923}}

Constanza Weber
{{PD-1923}}

Karl and Franz Mozart
Hans Hansen [Public domain]
{{PD-1923}}

Joseph Haydn
Thomas Hardy [Public domain]
{{PD-1923}}

Haydn playing in a string quartet
AnonymousUnknown author [Public domain]
{{PD-1923}}

The clarinet
Sotakeit at the English language Wikipedia [CC
BY-SA 3.0
(http://creativecommons.org/licenses/by-
sa/3.0/)]

**"Mozart's Last Days" - a painting by
Hermann von Kaulbach**
Hermann von Kaulbach [Public domain]
{{PD-1923}}

Made in the USA
Middletown, DE
17 March 2023